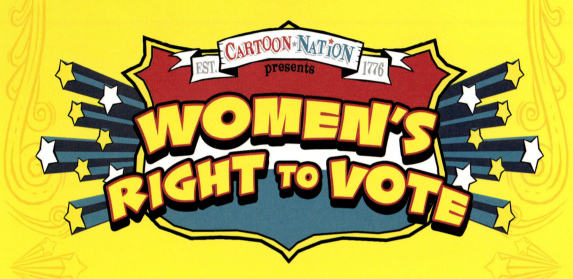

CARTOON·NATION presents

EST. 1776

WOMEN'S RIGHT TO VOTE

by Terry Collins

illustrated by Brian Bascle

CONSULTANT:

Sara M. Evans
Regents Professor Emerita
Department of History
University of Minnesota, Minneapolis

Capstone press

Mankato, Minnesota

Graphic Library is published by Capstone Press,
151 Good Counsel Drive, P.O. Box 669, Mankato, Minnesota 56002.
www.capstonepress.com

1 2 3 4 5 6 14 13 12 11 10 09

Library of Congress Cataloging-in-Publication Data
Collins, Terry.
    Women's right to vote / by Terry Collins; illustrated by Brian Bascle.
    p. cm. — (Graphic library. Cartoon nation)
    Includes bibliographical references and index.
    Summary: "In cartoon format, explains the history of the women's suffrage
movement" — Provided by publisher.
    ISBN-13: 978-1-4296-2341-4 (hardcover)
    ISBN-10: 1-4296-2341-1 (hardcover)
    1. Women — Suffrage — United States — History — Juvenile literature. I. Bascle,
Brian, ill. II. Title. III. Series.
JK1898.C65 2009
324.6'230973 — dc22   2008028695

Set Designer
Bob Lentz

Designer
Alison Thiele

Cover Artist
Kelly Brown

Editor
Lori Shores

Editor's note: Direct quotations from primary sources are indicated by a yellow background.

Direct quotations appear on the following pages:
Page 7, from the Liz Library, http://www.thelizlibrary.org/suffrage/abigail.htm
Page 9, from the Sojourner Truth Institute website, http://www.sojournertruth.org/Library/
    Speeches/AintIAWoman.htm
Page 13, from A History of the National Woman's Rights Movement by Paulina W. Davis,
    http://www.assumption.edu/whw/old/Davis_History.html
Page 17 (Anthony), from Divided Sisters, by Midge Wilson and Kathy Russell, http://condor.
    depaul.edu/~mwilson/divided/chptone.html
Page 17 (Truth), from the Sojourner Truth Institute website, http://www.sojournertruth.org/
    Library/Speeches/Default.htm
Page 21, from the Travel and History website, http://www.u-s-history.com/pages/h1080.html
Page 27, from the New York Times, http://www.nytimes.com/2008/06/07/us/politics/07text-
    clinton.html?fta=y

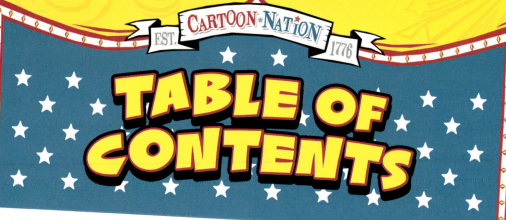

TABLE OF CONTENTS

EST. 1776 · CARTOON★NATION

DON'T FORGET TO VOTE

Every day, you face choices. What kind of cereal should you eat for breakfast? Who will you sit with at lunch? Should you use your allowance to buy ringtones for your cell phone, or save up for a new video game?

I can't make up my mind! I'm only a teenager!

Sometimes making the right decision is hard. However the choice is yours to make. Because the United States is a democracy, voters choose their leaders. All Americans have an equal right to have their voices heard in government.

Isn't democracy wonderful?

democracy — a form of government in which people choose their leaders

Voting is one of the most important rights given to Americans. This right allows people to choose the leaders who will make laws. Citizens who vote in a democracy are directly involved in the decisions of their government.

However, for women the right to vote came many years after the Constitution was written. Without the women's suffrage movement, voting today might look completely different.

suffrage — the right to vote

During the mid-1700s, the 13 colonies were ready for freedom. Rumblings of the American Revolution were being heard. At this time, the right to vote in local governments was limited to male property owners.

Many people believed that only the wealthy had the best interest in seeing a stable government. This idea did not allow poor people or women to vote. As such, only wealthy white men were allowed to make important decisions.

With the writing of the Declaration of Independence, America was on its way to becoming a new country. People had high hopes for the new government. Even Founding Father and future president John Adams couldn't ignore a growing demand to give women the right to vote. In fact, his wife, Abigail, was a believer in women's rights.

The passing of the Constitution in 1789 gave each state the right to decide who voted. All states refused to recognize women except for New Jersey. This state gave voting rights to "all free inhabitants," including women. Sadly, women's right to vote in New Jersey was taken away in 1807.

WOMEN SPEAK OUT

In the early 1800s, the role of women in America began to change. Women were becoming more educated. These ladies wanted their voices heard on important causes of the day.

The next thing you know, they'll be wearing pants.

One of these causes was the abolition movement to stop slave ownership. In the 1830s, women joined men as abolitionists and began to speak out against slavery. The sight of a woman protesting in public was very unusual, and for many, even shocking.

I say, that speaker, why is he wearing a dress?

Um, because she's a woman?

abolitionist — a person who worked to end slavery

Angelina and Sarah Grimke were the daughters of a South Carolina judge and slave owner. As adults, they spoke out against slavery. Angelina's anti-slavery article "An Appeal to the Christian Women of the South" was published in 1836. After the article, the sisters were threatened with arrest if they returned to their home state.

Happy Birthday, Dad!

It sure was easier to celebrate birthdays before we got kicked out of South Carolina!

You're telling me!

And ain't I a woman? Look at me! Look at my arm! I have ploughed, and planted, and gathered into barns, and no man could head me! And ain't I a woman?

Sojourner Truth (1797-1883), a freed slave, traveled the country to tell people her story. Sojourner also wrote her autobiography, *The Narrative of Sojourner Truth*. Sales of her life story supported her for the rest of her life as she continued to fight for the end of slavery.

Women realized they could make a difference in government and began to ask the obvious:

Why can't we vote?

In 1848, the first Women's Rights Convention was held in Seneca Falls, New York. Lucretia Mott and Elizabeth Cady Stanton organized the convention.

Mott and Stanton were old friends who teamed up to fight for equal rights. The pair would be involved in the battle for women's suffrage for decades.

Your new look will be a hit at the convention, Elizabeth!

I'm not sure, Lucretia.

The men and women who attended the convention discussed many topics. These included the idea that women should have equal rights in education, property ownership, and voting. Women who wanted to vote became known as suffragists.

You get an "A" for effort, but we're suffragists, not surf-ragists.

suffragist — a supporter of women's right to vote

At first, the idea of giving women the vote was not on the convention's agenda. Then Stanton suggested it. After a long talk, all agreed to make voting rights the top goal of the movement.

The convention ended with the group adopting a Declaration of Sentiments based on the Declaration of Independence. But writing the document did not make it become law. The fight for women's suffrage in America was just getting started.

DECLARATION OF SENTIMENTS

Some of the memorable quotes from the declaration include:

- We hold these truths to be self-evident, that all men and women are created equal.

- The history of mankind is a history of repeated injuries and usurpations on the part of man toward women.

- He has never permitted her to exercise her inalienable right to the elective franchise (to vote).

- He has compelled her to submit to law in the formation of which she had no voice.

- He has taken from her all right in property, even to the wages she earns.

Women's suffrage had much opposition, not just from men. Many women viewed the idea of "equal rights" as threatening the tradition of marriage.

Vote or marry? What shall I do?

You can do either one as long as all women get the right to vote!

The idea of shared responsibility for the family, as well as the house and decisions, was new to American men. While some men were willing to allow women to vote, other parts of equality made them nervous.

Let me get this straight. You want half of everything if we get married?

Half the money, half the house, half the land . . .

. . . and half of the responsibility for raising the children.

Foes of giving women the right to vote used silly reasons to keep men in power. The belief that males were smarter than females came up again and again. After all, doctors of the era insisted that women had "smaller brains."

A husband and wife should be equal partners in everything.

Sure, sure. Whatever you say, honey.

Poor thing. Look at the size of her tiny brain!

Men also feared that if women spent all of their time studying, life at home would fall apart. If women traveled or followed politics, what would happen to the American family? Who would care for the children?

A little help here, please?

In a moment, dear. I want to finish this chapter first.

ELIZABETH CADY STANTON

When the women's rights group met in 1850, no men served as leaders. Instead, women dominated the meeting. Men stayed involved in the suffrage movement, but women took control of their own destiny.

For the first time in the world's history, men learned how it felt to sit in silence when questions in which they had an interest were discussed.

The first National Women's Rights Convention met in Worcester, Massachusetts, in 1850. More than 1,000 people from 11 states attended. The convention led to an eight-state petition drive to give women the right to vote.

MASSACHUSETTS

petition – a written request signed by many people asking those in power to change a policy

Volunteers tried to gain 150 supporters from each state represented, but they met with no success. Still people heard about the cause. Newspapers promoted suffrage, even when criticizing the idea. The belief that women should be given a voice wasn't going away.

Such events did not escape the notice of Susan B. Anthony. The former teacher was active in a movement to outlaw the sale of alcohol. Tired of being told to sit quietly and learn from the men in charge, Anthony formed the all-women Daughters of Temperance.

Susan, where are you going?

Anywhere but here! I'm tired of being ignored!

temperance — moderation or self-control, especially with regard to alcohol

After meeting Elizabeth Cady Stanton in 1851, Anthony joined the suffrage moment. Anthony became the movement's spokesperson, traveling to spread the message. Now women from across the country began to speak out wherever a group could be gathered.

Miss Anthony, our readers want to know why you are so serious. Can't you smile for the camera?

Sir, if you want a smile, help me get women the right to vote.

A DOLLAR TRIBUTE

Susan B. Anthony was the first woman to be honored by having her likeness placed on United States money. On July 2, 1979, the U.S. Mint released the coin. The debut of the *Anthony dollar* was in Rochester, N.Y. Rochester was the suffragist's home during the most politically active years of her life.

Progress in getting women's suffrage was put on hold from 1861 to 1865 during the Civil War. However, the end of the war brought new laws, new ideas, and a chance for equal rights for everyone.

WOMEN'S RIGHT TO VOTE

RIGHT TO VOTE

Universal suffrage for all!

Women of all races and African American men worked together as a team. They pushed for voting rights for all, no matter their gender or skin color.

The 14th Amendment to the Constitution was passed in 1868. It granted citizenship and the right to vote to all men age 21 or older. This was soon followed by the 15th Amendment to protect the civil rights of African American men.

> I will cut off this right arm of mine before I will ever work for or demand the ballot for the Negro and not the woman!

> Is she always this dramatic?

In both amendments, women were left out. Those women who fought for suffrage for all felt betrayed. Suffragists would have to work harder now to get the right to vote. Even Sojourner Truth called for the right of all women — black or white — to vote.

> Why children, if you have woman's rights, give it to her and you will feel better.

Tired of fighting among themselves, the leaders of the women's right to vote movement split in 1869. Elizabeth Cady Stanton and Susan B. Anthony formed the National Woman Suffrage Association (NWSA) in New York. Others organized the American Woman Suffrage Association (AWSA) in Boston.

While the mission of both groups was similar, the approach was different. The NWSA demanded a national amendment to the Constitution. The AWSA was quieter. They wanted to get voting rights for women on a state-by-state basis.

If I had known I could just walk in and vote, I would have done it years ago!

In the 1872 presidential elections, women in several states tried to cast their votes. One of these women was Susan B. Anthony. She showed up to place her ballot for Ulysses S. Grant. Surprisingly, election officials allowed her to go ahead and vote.

So, what are you in for?

Voting illegally.

I better keep my distance!

Two weeks later, Anthony was arrested by a U.S. Marshal and charged with "illegal voting." She used this arrest to promote suffrage. Before the trial, Anthony traveled the country to tell her side of the story.

At the trial, Judge Ward Hunt would not let Anthony talk in court because she was a woman. He ordered her to pay a $100 fine. When finally allowed to speak, Anthony said, "May it please your honor, I shall never pay a dollar of your unjust penalty." She never paid the fine.

Miss Anthony, while I told you not to speak, I hardly think a gag is necessary.

After the Civil War, alcohol sales increased. Worried wives noticed the impact of alcohol abuse on the home and the family. Women who had never thought of voting joined a new cause — the abolishment of the sale of liquor. This battle became known as "The Woman's War."

These women, many from wealthy families, protested outside saloons and liquor stores. Their methods got results. Between 1873 and 1874, about 3,000 saloons were closed throughout the United States.

Led by Frances E. Willard, the Women's Christian Temperance Union (WCTU) tried to tie female suffrage into the movement to ban alcohol. After all, if women could vote, they could use legal means to stop the spread of liquor.

Temperance is moderation in the things that are good and total abstinence from the things that are foul.

WCTU
FRANCES WILLARD, PRESIDENT

FRANCES WILLARD

What did she say?

Be a good person and never drink.

Never?!

Men believed if women voted, they would end alcohol sales for good. Because of this, local officials and the liquor industry opposed laws giving women more rights. By the time the suffragists realized what was happening, it was too late.

Well, it seemed like a good idea at the time.

Good grief!

THE FORGOTTEN FEMINIST

While many people today have never heard of Frances Willard, her efforts for women's rights mark her place in history. Willard promoted sports for women, and even became the founding president of Northwestern Ladies College. She also worked to ban the sale of illegal drugs across the world. At her death in 1898, she was one of the most famous women in America.

By the late 1800s, the idea of women's suffrage was no longer new. In 1878, U.S. Senator A. A. Sargent introduced the Anthony Amendment into Congress. The uphill battle to make equal voting rights for all had begun.

As time passed, so did grudges. Younger women joined the battle for the vote and saw the strength of their growing numbers. The existing suffrage groups joined to form a united front — the National American Woman Suffrage Association (NAWSA).

As America entered the 1900s, more women entered the workforce. These pioneers worked under dangerous conditions for low pay. In 1910, female factory workers went on strike in New York City. They also helped arrange the first women's suffrage parade. Hundreds of women showed up to march.

In 1913, President Woodrow Wilson met with Alice Paul, a social worker. Paul had recently opened a Washington office known as the Woman's Party to support voting rights. Paul urged the president to give women the right to vote.

Paul also helped to spread word of the cause. By July 1913, 531 Americans presented a petition to President Wilson. The petition had more than 200,000 signatures supporting women's suffrage.

When the United States entered World War I in 1917, the role of women in America changed once again. Overseas, they served as nurses, secretaries, and office workers. At home, they filled tough physical jobs left open when men were sent to fight.

I can work a 12-hour shift in a hospital, but I still can't vote? Come on, already!

President Wilson knew the time had come to grant women the vote. The country was ready to make things right. On September 30, 1918, he asked legislators to reconsider the Anthony Amendment that dated back to 1878.

Ah-choo!

Sorry, this one is a little dusty.

The Anthony Amendment lost by two votes, but Wilson didn't give up. On May 19, 1919, he called a special session of the House of Representatives for another vote. This time the House agreed, and the Senate followed.

On June 4, 1919, the 19th Amendment was passed. States voted the amendment into law on August 26, 1920. About 26 million women voted for the first time in their lives in the November 1920 election.

WOMEN IN GOVERNMENT

After the 19th Amendment became law, the role of women in American government grew. With the power of the vote, women made an impact on laws and who was elected. Better still, women could now run for public office on a local, state, or federal level.

As the decades passed, women were elected to the United States Senate and House of Representatives.

In 1984, Walter "Fritz" Mondale was the Democratic nominee for president. He named Geraldine Ferraro as his running mate for vice president. The Mondale/Ferraro ticket lost, but Ferraro still made history as the first female vice presidential nominee.

In 2008, Senator Hillary Rodham Clinton ran for president of the United States. The former first lady became a leading nominee for the Democratic Party. Clinton took many states, but realized she could not win enough votes for the nomination. She dropped out of the race on June 7.

SENATOR CLINTON LIVE FROM WASHINGTON D.C.

Although we weren't able to shatter that highest, hardest glass ceiling this time, thanks to you, it's got about 18 million cracks in it.

During her final speech, she spoke proudly about how far women have come in American politics. She honored her millions of supporters by saying:

glass ceiling — slang term for an invisible barrier that prevents women from getting higher positions of leadership

That same glass ceiling received an additional crack on August 29, 2008. Sarah Palin, the governor of Alaska, was named as the vice presidential candidate for the Republican Party.

I'm ready to go, John! Where do you want to start campaigning?

H-H-How about H-H-H-Hawaii?

The McCain/Palin ticket lost, but Palin made history as the first female vice presidential Republican nominee.

TIME LINE

1848 — The first women's rights convention is held in Seneca Falls, New York.

1850 — First National Women's Rights Convention is held in Worcester, Massachusetts.

1850

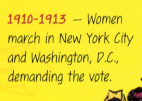

1848

1878 — The Anthony Amendment is introduced into the U.S. Congress, but is unsuccessful. It would have given women the right to vote.

1910-1913 — Women march in New York City and Washington, D.C., demanding the vote.

1878

1910-1913

1920 — The 19th Amendment is signed into law, giving women the right to vote.

1920

1851 — Sojourner Truth delivers her famous "Ain't I A Woman?" speech in Akron, Ohio.

1851

1869 — The newly formed Wyoming territory passes a law allowing women to vote.

1869

1872 — Susan B. Anthony is arrested for "illegal voting."

1872

1984 — Geraldine Ferraro is named as the vice-presidential running mate of Democratic presidential candidate Walter Mondale.

1984

2008 — Hillary Rodham Clinton seeks the Democratic nomination for president of the United States.

2008

GLOSSARY

abolitionist (ab-uh-LI-shuhn-ist) — a person who worked to end slavery

amendment (uh-MEND-muhnt) — a change made to a law or a legal document

convention (kuhn-VEN-shuhn) — a large gathering of people who have the same interests

democracy (di-MOK-ruh-see) — a form of government in which people choose their leaders

glass ceiling (GLAS SEE-ling) — slang term for an invisible barrier that prevents women from getting higher positions of leadership

petition (puh-TISH-uhn) — a written request signed by many people asking those in power to change a policy

suffrage (SUHF-rij) — the right to vote

suffragist (SUHF-ri-jist) — a supporter of women's right to vote

temperance (TEM-puh-runss) — moderation or self-control, especially with regard to alcohol

unalienable (uhn-AY-lee-uhn-uh-buhl) — unable to be taken away from or given away

usurpation (yoo-sur-PAY-shuhn) — the forceful taking of a position of power or rights

READ MORE

Burgan, Michael. *The 19th Amendment.* We the People. Minneapolis: Compass Point Books, 2006.

Macbain-Stephens, Jennifer. *Women's Suffrage: Giving the Right to Vote to All Americans.* The Progressive Movement, 1900-1920 — Efforts to Reform America's New Industrial Society. New York: Rosen, 2006.

Rau, Dana Meachen. *Great Women of the Suffrage Movement.* We the People. Minneapolis: Compass Point Books, 2006.

Stone, Tanya Lee. *Elizabeth Leads the Way: Elizabeth Cady Stanton and the Right to Vote.* New York: Henry Holt, 2008.

INTERNET SITES

FactHound offers a safe, fun way to find educator-approved Internet sites related to this book.

Here's what you do:

1. Visit *www.facthound.com*
2. Choose your grade level.
3. Begin your search.

This book's ID number is 9781429623414.

FactHound will fetch the best sites for you!

INDEX